Essential Preparation for

UMAT

UNDERGRADUATE MEDICINE & HEALTH SCIENCES ADMISSION TEST

Series Three

2

BOOK 2
UNDERSTANDING PEOPLE

Mohan Dhall

Five Senses Education Pty Ltd
2/195 Prospect Highway
Seven Hills 2147
New South Wales
Australia

Dhall, Mohan
Series 3, Book 2 - Understanding People

ISBN 978-1-76032-007-2

CONTENTS

Introduction to UMAT Testing   Page 4

Understanding People Questions   Page 7

Answers   Page 31

Multiple Choice Answer Sheets   Page 47

Introduction to UMAT and the Trial Test Papers

Students can gain access into medical training in Australia in one of three ways:

- Through post-graduate entry following the completion of an undergraduate degree. This degree should be in science or science related subjects and the student will need to achieve a high Grade Point Average (GPA).

- Through direct entry based on Year 12 results

- Through performance on the UMAT test and interview (done by each participating university, depending on UMAT results)

The purpose of the UMAT entry test is to assist in the selection of candidates who display the requisite thinking skills and abilities for successful medical training. The test is a 3-hour test completed under exam conditions. There are 134 questions based around three different types of thinking and reasoning:

1. Logical reasoning and problem-solving (48 questions)
2. Understanding people skills (44 questions)
3. Non-verbal reasoning (42 questions)

The follow-up interview performed by participating universities can be quite demanding and can take up to an hour, before a panel of up to three interviewers. Thus preparation and the development of appropriate interview skills and techniques should be practiced, in addition to undertaking test-training.

UMAT Understanding People Questions

There are 44 practice questions here

Students should aim to take about 55 minutes to complete them. There are practice answer sheets at the end of this book. Try not to mark the pages, as you will be able to repeat the questions and test yourself several times.

Instructions to candidates

These questions assess the ability of students to understand and reason about people. Questions are based on scenario, dialogue, observations or other text representing specific interpersonal situations.

The questions will assess your ability to identify, understand, and where necessary infer the thoughts, feelings and behaviour and/or intentions of the people represented in the situations.

Interpersonal Understanding is an ability considered important for anyone intending to work as a medical or health professional. Increasingly, patients, health professionals and the community are recognising that to treat people effectively, doctors and health workers need a high level of personal interaction skills and ability. Questions are generally based on texts or scenarios that feature personal reflections or interpersonal situations. Some passages may involve interactions between health professionals and patients, but they are not confined to health settings. No specialised knowledge is expected. The questions test a candidate's ability to identify, understand and, where necessary, infer the thoughts, feelings, behaviour and/or intentions of the people represented in the situations.

© Mohan Dhall
© Five Senses Education Pty Ltd

Understanding People
Questions

Questions 1 – 3

This is a recount from a 68-year-old man who took his 91-year-old father to a surgeon. The father was in need of surgery but the risks were quite high.

Though my father was with me, the surgeon was quite blunt and rude to him. The surgeon said, "The surgery you need is very serious – but don't worry. I'm an expert! I know there are cheaper options but at your age I would go with the surgery I recommend. You know – as we get older the risks are greater so money really should not be your main consideration...' When my father tried to speak, the surgeon spoke over him in a harsh tone and said, "no second opinion is needed in your case, because surgery is the best option and as, it turns out, I am the expert at the type of surgery needed..."

So, I sat quietly beside my father, raging inside. Then after he had spoken to my father I said, *"Can I just go back through what you said"*. I took out a note pad and pen and started to write things down. I did a couple of units of law at university so I said, *"With my legal training..."* I noticed the doctor suddenly stiffen and take interest. So I continued. *"With my legal training I know how important it is to get things really clear"*. Within seconds the surgeon had totally changed. He became incredibly accommodating, offered choices to my father and even followed up later with a phone call. Suddenly everything seemed cheaper and surgery really wasn't necessary. I hate it when surgeons try and take advantage of the elderly or those they think they can baffle...

Question 1

What is the attitude of the surgeon?

A) Self-protective
B) Self-serving
C) Arrogant
D) Demeaning

Question 2

What is the son's role with respect to his father?

A) Patron
B) Mentor
C) Leader
D) Advocate

Question 3

Why does the surgeon's attitude change?

A) He thinks he has met his match in a lawyer
B) He believes he is about to get in trouble
C) He thinks the son is a legal expert
D) He knows that he has acted recklessly

Questions 4 - 7

"I just want to push my son", she said to me. Her son, she said, was not like his older brother. The older brother was in Year 11 and doing so well in the academically selective school. Surely the younger boy should be the same?

After one session of tutoring my special needs tutor reported that the young boy had learning difficulties. The mother refused to believe it and, in tears, said that this could not be true. She needed her son to be bright because that would mean he could go to a good school and not the local school. The mother refused to have the special needs tutor help her son and asked if I could give a second opinion. It was evident as he read aloud to me that boy's reading was very poor with obvious pronunciation errors such as substituting 'f' for 'th' and reading 'three' as 'free', 'the' as 'duh' and 'although' as 'aldough'. Apart from this error, and a failure to stop at full stops, the reading was quite slow and disjointed.

I recommended that the mother have the boy psychometrically assessed so that any tutoring and also any teaching through school could be properly informed. She was reluctant. Surely her son just needed to "work hard". The cost of the testing was waived so that any issue of cost was not a factor.

The psychometric test revealed that the boy was well below average (bottom 3%) in terms of reading comprehension. However his spelling was in the 99th percentile. He had a very short working memory. This type of psychometric profile clearly indicates learning difficulties.

At this point the mother seemed to accept that she needed to make decisions about her son that matched his ability. However, this was only temporary. By the end of the week she had him do several more reading tasks and purchased copies of books for preparation for the selective schools exam. I suggested that she have him read aloud for twenty minutes a day to improve his literacy and we commenced free weekly one and a half hour sessions of reading comprehension. The mother said her own command of English was so poor she could not have him read to her.

It was during the holidays in one of these sessions that I asked the boy how he would spend the rest of his day. The boy said, "at my muder work". When I later inquired of the mother she said that every day of the holidays he had spent all day at work learning with her. He had not seen any friends, saw no movies and did not play computer games at all in the two weeks.

A week later when we had a session together the boy got just over half of the fifty items correct. When his mother was being shown the work he would smile when she saw the correct responses but would closely read her face when she saw his incorrect responses. I commented that the boy appeared to be tying his self-esteem to her approval and disapproval around the success of his answers. He nodded when I said this and she looked down.

A day later I received a phone call from the mother. In it she stated that she would no longer be bringing her son to tutoring as her "shift times had changed". I suggested times outside of her altered shift times but she refused saying, "I still want to push him. All he has to do is stop being lazy".

Question 4

How does the mother feel about her oldest son?

A) Like he is a success and the role-model for other children
B) That he should work harder and be as smart as possible
C) If he is lazy he will go to the wrong school
D) That he is successful because he is in a selective school

Question 5

How does the mother feel about her ability in English?

A) Uncertain
B) Under-confident
C) Useless
D) Undecided

Question 6

Why was the cost of the testing waived?

A) The author sensed the mother may find any excuse to avoid knowing
B) The mother needed to see the value before she would pay
C) The son needed to save because the testing would be expensive
D) The author sought to make it free in order to win the mother's trust

Question 7

What does the author seek to convey through this piece?

A) A sense of bewilderment
B) A sense of hope
C) A sense of enthusiasm
D) A sense of loss

Questions 8 - 9

The following is a conversation between Josie and Mark, a couple who have been dating for a couple of months.

Mark: Did you get the card and flowers I sent...?

Josie: I've been thinking of you...

Mark: I have been wondering whether you care...?

Josie: I do... but I prefer face-to-face talking.

Mark: You will be away for 6 weeks...

Josie: I want you to write to me.

Mark: Do you promise me you'll reply? It's hard having a one-sided conversation.

Josie: I know I have been too quiet.

Mark: You need to break the walls.

Josie: I might just lower them a little...

Question 8

How does Mark feel through this conversation?

A) Alone and afraid
B) Confused and uncertain
C) Hurt and angry
D) Alert and used

Question 9

What does Josie's comment "I might just lower them a little..." reveal?

A) She likes to be in control of her emotions
B) She is too guarded to get close to Mark
C) She is afraid of hurting Mark again
D) She does not mind learning to be vulnerable

Question 10 - 12

> **Matt:** I can't run mate. My knees are shot and I'm getting old.
> **Greig:** (Exasperated) Age isn't a function of time! It's a function of the mind.
> **Matt:** Nah... I tried to jog once recently – but it hurt.
> **Greig:** Did you try again the next day? Did you experiment to see what would happen?
> **Matt:** I'm not you mate. I'm looking forward to not trying any more. Life is too short not to eat and drink and take it easy. Besides, everyone knows running is bad for your knees.
> **Greig:** Have you ever seen what's on the other side of pain? You have no idea! Recent medical and scientific research demonstrates that running overcomes arthritis. Living a lazy life is what kills!
> **Matt:** Who you calling lazy? I work harder than anyone I know. Only an idiot wouldn't know that.
> **Greig:** Only an idiot would give up before trying. There is a time to start and a time to stop. Of course, things can be overdone – but they can also be underdone...
> **Matt:** I didn't give up. I'm just not interested. Now back off.
> **Greig:** When you are ready to start living – call me. (Walks off shaking his head)

Question 10

How can the discussion between Matt and Greig be best described?

A) Tense
B) Angry
C) Spirited
D) Unfulfilled

Question 11

Which word best describes how Greig views Matt?

A) Feisty
B) Thoughtless
C) Sleepy
D) Indolent

Question 12

Which statement can be attributed to Greig?

A) "I don't like training or gym-work"
B) "My goal is to run a 15-kilometre race"
C) "I will never give up! I will never die!"
D) "All forms of pain are bad, but some are worse than others"

© Mohan Dhall
© Five Senses Education Pty Ltd

Questions 13 - 15

The following is a recount from a Sydney resident of a siege initiated by an Islamic extremist that took place in the city centre and resulted in the death of two hostages.

The siege made me angry. It was an attack on my city. It made the city unsafe and I cried afterwards. Boy, did I cry. My friends and I went to city and laid flowers for the two hostages who died. I think they should re-name Martin Place, "Peace Square" because we are a peace-loving nation of diverse people and diverse values, where people co-exist peacefully.

They will place a plaque close to the site of the siege on the first anniversary. They will make a small garden. I wonder whether that's enough. I saw the sea of flowers and felt the spontaneous outpouring of emotion in the days after the siege. As I lay my flowers down I saw a small boy holding a card. The card read, "Good bye Tori and Katrina. We will always love you". His father's face was still, eyes lowered and the mood was sombre.

Even now, a month later, I catch my breath and divert my thoughts if something reminds me of that awful, terrible day. I don't think I will ever get over it.

Question 13

Why does the author say, "The siege made me angry"?

A) She felt a loss of control
B) She felt like her city was being invaded
C) She thought there would be future sieges
D) She was deeply disappointed

Question 14

What feeling makes the author divert her thoughts?

A) Sadness
B) Loss
C) Anxiety
D) Overwhelmed

Question 15

Which is **not** an alternative for the word "sombre"?

A) Effusive
B) Melancholy
C) Sober
D) Mournful

Questions 16 - 17

The following is an excerpt from a discussion between a young man Sam, and his father.

"I'm really not sure what to do. The work as an apprentice pays so poorly for forty and a half hours per week. This is longer than the 38-hour week I did in retail and it also means that I am not paid for overtime.

Today I had to dig a fifteen metre long trench for cables. It was rainy and wet and I feel buggered. After that I had to crawl under the building for about forty metres. It was so low I could not lift my head. I had to push through the spider webs and it was awful. To get out I had to crawl backwards on my stomach.

I think a retail job would pay better and be less demeaning.

As regards my lunch break. I get there at 8AM and we are asked to take lunch at 11AM. That makes the afternoon shift 11:30AM to 5PM. They only give us half an hour, and even that can be disrupted. This job is such a bugger."

Question 16

What is Sam feeling?

A) Angry
B) Dispirited
C) Sad
D) Lonely

Question 17

What does a retail job represent to Sam?

A) A reality check
B) An opportunity
C) An escape
D) An exciting change

Questions 18 - 20

The following is an extract from a man's diary recounting the evening following a break up with the partner he thought he would be marrying.

There it was. Over before it had even seemed to start. As the rain fell and I made my way home from the airport I wondered what had happened. How was it possible for me to fall so completely for someone, who encouraged the contact, communication and closeness only for her to withdraw so quickly? How was it that in my head I saw us laugh together in the taxi, on her back step, at the party, on the street through Newtown as we walked home, at the street café in Singapore? How was it she was so open and then so totally closed? Surely she's recalling the same things? The things that made her tell everyone I'm the one – where did that go? And why doesn't she answer my calls, text or Skype or tell me what she's thinking?

I heard her say that she needed to focus on her work, wanted to be selfish, found herself falling and didn't want to not rise. As if I would let her let herself down. As if I would not give her space. As if I am her past that crowded and bruised her.

Question 18

What do the questions at the end of the first paragraph suggest about the author?

A) He is trying to find the truth in a situation where there was lies
B) He is seeking understanding where there is confusion
C) He is seeking calmness because he feels very upset
D) He is trying to catch up with the present and feels left behind

Question 19

What does the rain represent?

A) Washing away of the relationship
B) The uncertainty of the situation
C) Drowning in sorrow and self-pity
D) The sadness of the change

Question 20

Which word best describes the feeling evoked by the line *"As if I am her past that crowded and bruised her"*?

A) Compassion
B) Difference
C) Hurt
D) Protective

Questions 21 - 23

The following is a discussion between two women about communication with their children.

Nora: With Facebook and Instagram I can watch my kids anywhere, anytime.

Pinky: You are on Facebook so you can catch up with your children? That's creepy!

Nora: Yeah – I have girls so I watch them closely...

Pinky: Girls? You mean a 25-year-old and a 22-year-old...? Give them space to grow up!

Nora: You wouldn't understand. We chat eight times a day. You could say we are a close family.

Pinky: Close? You can't even get your work done because every minute it's your sister on the phone, or your mother or one of your daughters. Sounds stifling to me!

Nora: You wouldn't know close - given your kids left home when they got to uni.

Question 21

Nora's parenting style may be characterised as

A) close and loving
B) protective and caring
C) controlling and dependent
D) caring and limiting

Question 22

Pinky is best described as

A) observant
B) opinionated
C) passionate
D) aggressive

Question 23

This statement by Nora: "You wouldn't know close - given your kids left home when they got to uni" shows that she is feeling

A) pressured
B) defensive
C) open
D) attacked

Questions 24 - 25

This is a recount by a young man, Adam, who survived a very serious car accident that left him with permanent leg injuries, and from which he was lucky to survive.

"I will never forget the smell of fuel and hot metal with burnt rubber and smoke. The glass everywhere, the stillness, the wail of sirens…. Once we were crashing I shut my eyes and waited. Everything slowed down and time felt different. The smash into the huge fence post that shattered the left side of the car brought me back. Time suddenly was in real-time and the glass, smoke and stillness were palpable in the mid-winter coldness. I breathed out fog and blood – a strange mix that spelt on my face and in the air, 'l-u-c-k-y-t-o-b-e-a-l-i-v-e' but at the time that brought pain into my face and mouth, aches all over my body, the reality of losing my car and nearly losing my life… the shock of the suddenness of uncontrolled change.

A few weeks ago, at night, I heard a screech and crash outside my house. I ran, fearing the worst. I got to the car first and straight away smelt that smell: fuel, hot metal, burnt rubber and smoke. Made me stop for a moment. Then I had to act quickly to free the driver. Throughout though I was in two places at once, fearing the worst and working for the best."

Question 24

What would Adam have felt when he heard the sound of the car crash?

A) A mix of concern and confidence
B) Ambivalence about whether to help or not
C) Both trepidation and fear
D) Numbness and loss simultaneously

Question 25

Which word best describes Adam's feeling in respect of the accident he had?

A) Sorrow
B) Relief
C) Restlessness
D) Angst

© Mohan Dhall
© Five Senses Education Pty Ltd

Question 26 - 28

This is a phone discussion between 45-year-old Brent and his 43-year-old sister, Zephyr, on his birthday.

Zephyr: Happy Birthday, bro! I hope you have a great day!

Brent: Thanks! That was unexpected! It's been a quiet morning.

Zephyr: So – doing anything special today?

Brent: Um – don't think so. As you know, Julia's away and she hasn't called yet...

Zephyr: Oh never mind about her. Do something for yourself. Now tell me: what would you like me to get you? Just tell me and I will get it.

Brent: Um... I don't think like that. I never ask for things and feel strange requesting something. If you want to get me something then just do so.

Zephyr: I just don't want to get you something you won't use or like. What do you want?

Brent: I don't want anything except warm communication. I prefer that to material symbols. Remember? I said that last year, the year before and the year before that...

Zephyr: Okay – but just let me know okay? So, when will you hear from Julia...? Is she still not talking to you? She must be pretty upset with you...

Brent: Zephyr! Why did you call?

© Mohan Dhall
© Five Senses Education Pty Ltd

Question 26

What is the difference in the way Brent and Zephyr communicate?

A) Brent is reflective, Zephyr is impulsive
B) Brent is reactive, Zephyr is inquisitive
C) Brent is passive, Zephyr is active
D) Brent is insightful, Zephyr is persistent

Question 27

What sentiment is Zephyr expressing when offering to buy Brent a present?

A) Zephyr is interested in Brent knowing that she's thinking of him
B) Zephyr is keen to be seen to do the right thing by Brent
C) Zephyr wants to feel like she is needed by Brent by helping him
D) Zephyr is buying time because she forgot to get Brent a present

Question 28

What is Brent feeling when he says, "Remember?"

A) Undervalued
B) Objectified
C) Angry
D) Sad

Questions 29 - 31

The following excerpt comes from an interview with a full-time carer, Lydia* of her daughter who has a profound disability. Her daughter is now 19-years-old and is totally dependent on her mother. (* Name has been changed)

"The National Disability Insurance Scheme (NDIS) has been amazing. It provides a framework for proper financial support for the first time. But there is a ridiculous amount of paperwork and accountability. I have to keep receipts for all the therapists, need to allocate hours each week accounting for every dollar and every cent. Don't get me wrong – I think accountability is important, but wouldn't mind if it was a bit easier and I could spend more time with my daughter. Ever since she was born people have not looked at me the same way. They look at me as though I am lesser and like I don't belong. That has been quite a battle because it means if I advocate I am seen as a stirrer or troublemaker. If I ask a teacher what was done in the special school I am labelled as a 'pushy-parent'. But who wouldn't want what's best for their child? And why should a child who cannot speak or see be denied basic rights such as an education?"

Question 29

How does Lydia feel about the NDIS?

A) Ambivalent
B) Happy
C) Unsettled
D) Upset

Question 30

As a carer, what does Lydia experience from others when she advocates for her daughter?

A) Subtle discrimination
B) Overt exclusion
C) Name calling
D) Unmitigated support

Question 31

Which of the following best describes Lydia's support for her daughter?

A) Unnecessarily forthright
B) Lazily passive
C) Surprisingly accepting
D) Appropriately strong

Questions 32 – 34

This is a recount from a mother, Helga*, who is struggling to make 'ends meet'.

"I couldn't afford the Catholic school for the three children. They have to go to the public schools. Little Ophelia* needs another test to assess her cognition and I'm not sure how she will cope with school. The eldest, Isadora*, is angry all the time now that she is going through hormonal changes associated with getting her periods. Terrence*, the middle one, needs new shoes but will never say anything. He's so compliant I worry I might overlook him and no-one will ever notice him. Anyway, the car broke down and the kids had to wait for a friend to pick them up. And with winter coming I'm not sure how I will afford to buy them warm clothes and heat the house. I would take a second job but then I'd be too tired to properly look after the kids. Feels like I have nothing and no choices."

* All names have been changed

Question 32

Which word best describes Helga's feeling with respect to Ophelia?

A) Hopeful
B) Loss
C) Uncertainty
D) Aggravation

Question 33

How does Helga feel about Terrence's quietness and compliance?

A) Fiery
B) Defensive
C) Angry
D) Watchful

Question 34

How does Helga view her present situation?

A) Helpless
B) Hopeless
C) Restrictive
D) Energising

Questions 35 - 37

Two women, Debbie and Josette* are discussing the issue of breast-feeding in public. (* Not their real names)

Debbie:	I cannot understand all of the fuss. Breastfeeding is natural and real.
Josette:	I think that it is a private matter between a mother and her child or children. It is not appropriate to be on public display.
Debbie:	Well, do you have a problem with babies drinking from a bottle in public? A hungry child needs to be fed, and a woman's body should not be a source of disgust.
Josette:	It just isn't appropriate. What next? Topless women driving buses?
Debbie:	You cannot be serious. What is inappropriate about a woman feeding her baby in public or in private? Why would anyone have a problem with that?
Josette:	Will you be advocating for public sex next?
Debbie:	(Horrified) What? There is nothing sexual about feeding a baby. Moreover, the sexualisation of the female body should not be something complicating the decision. For bonding reasons and for health reasons it is so much more appropriate to breastfeed than bottlefeed. It provides far greater immunity for the child. How can that be a problem?
Josette:	The issue isn't breastfeeding *per se*....it's breastfeeding in public. Surely a woman who respects herself should leave that to the privacy of her home. She shouldn't force others to have to put up with her flashing all over the place...
Debbie:	So a woman should be able to breastfeed – just not in public? That seems like a ridiculous double standard!
Josette:	Well, everybody knows that modesty is an appropriate standard for women. These days everybody wants to put 'me' first and to hell with everything and everyone else.
Debbie:	Modesty? Again – this is about the baby not the mother wanting to show off. What is the matter with you? People like you need to be less uptight about a fairly basic human right.
Josette:	Human rights extend to those who have to watch the disgusting behaviour of others!

Question 35

Josette's attitude towards breastfeeding is that

A) it is fine but lowers the standard of society when done in public
B) should be confined to the home as it is offensive elsewhere
C) it is never okay to breastfeed, particularly in public
D) it demeans women and their bodies

Question 36

Why does Josette say, "Well, everybody knows that modesty is an appropriate standard for women."?

A) She understands widespread public opinion and seeks to convey it
B) She is angry and want the support of a broader group
C) She wants to strengthen her argument by referring to an external standard
D) She thinks that it should be obvious to Debbie that she (Josette) is right

Question 37

How would Debbie's tone and language be characterised?

A) Flippant and thoughtful
B) Focused and persuasive
C) Caring and concerned
D) Argumentative and aggressive

Questions 38 - 40

The following is a recount by an elite sportsman about competition, training and pain.

There was always pain. It didn't matter if it was during the drills at training or during a game – something would always hurt. The thing is, you learnt never to show pain. That is the nature of competition. You learn to mask injury and pain because the opponent will exploit any perceived weakness. This means that if you got struck by the ball and it fractured a rib you didn't rub the injury. If you fell awkwardly and hurt your shoulder you got up, flexed and stretched – but hid the grimace.

Injuries in training are very annoying because the idea is to train to strength. Overtraining can be an issue so careful monitoring is important. It is also crucial not to let pain or injury dominate, as often training through pain and injury help in the recovery. A person soon learns to distinguish between 'good' pain and 'bad' pain. Being active, when the body wants to rest, or when the mind is stalling is very important. To do your best you cannot compromise on knowing your body, managing pain and injury, and focusing on the goal.

Question 38

Why does the author say that sportspeople should hide their pain?

A) It looks stronger and men are meant to be strong
B) Hiding pain helps a person to focus on what they need to do to win the game
C) Real men do not cry
D) So that a weakness cannot be taken advantage of

Question 39

Which is the best word to describe the sportsman?

A) Determined
B) Helpful
C) Selfish
D) Intuitive

Question 40

What is the relationship between pain and competition?

A) Competing is painful because people can lose and be disappointed
B) Pain is the competition because those who manage pain best win
C) Competition brings pain and pain is to be masked when it arrives
D) Pain is a part of competition and without it there would be no competition

Questions 41 - 42

Two women are discussing a situation where one of the women sent an email to her whole work department but accidentally copied it to someone she had insulted in the email.

Tickie*:	Ooops – that didn't go quite as I'd planned.
Betty*:	Haha – you sure know how to get yourself into a beautiful mess!
Tickie:	I – um, I – that will be awkward next time I see Jenny*.
Betty:	Yeah – I think it would have really hurt her. It was quite mean.
Tickie:	Well, in a way she deserved it...but I'd have preferred she didn't get the email.
Betty:	Well, at least she now knows what you _really_ think!
Tickie:	(Pausing) Hmmm...I guess it is a bit more complicated than that.
Betty:	I don't think so. You owe her no apologies.

*The names have been changed

Question 41

How did Tickie feel when the person she had insulted read the email?

A) Delighted
B) Exposed
C) Satisfied
D) Disappointed

Question 42

What is Betty's role in the conversation?

A) Supportive
B) Critical
C) Confusing
D) Neutral

Questions 43 - 44

This is the diary entry of Nancy*, a woman in her early 60s who was writing about her experience of aging.

I first noticed that my sight changed. I saw myself holding things further away in order to see them properly – the text messages on the mobile phone were increasingly difficult to read. I had seen others do that, but never even considered why until I found myself doing it.

Then I noticed that my veins changed – they seemed somehow to thicken. I also found that my memory was changing and I needed to have reminders and make sure everything was alarmed.

But worst of all is this pervasive feeling of pending loss. I live alone now, having been a single mum for 35 years, but the children left long ago to live their own lives with their own partners. So the house is quiet and I wonder what time has become. All I really have is a combination of memories and a measure of satisfaction that my children are happy and they did not suffer unduly for my failings and limitations.

But in the quiet of night, after darkness has settled, I wonder how it will end. Will the darkness simply creep into me, extending my sleep? Will there be a dramatic daylight departure from an accident? Or will I feel some pain that creeps through me, accelerating over time, as I lose grip and wish for stillness and silence from the hurting?

*Not her real name

Question 43

When she reviews her life Nancy would feel which of the following?

A) Regretful
B) Reassured
C) Restless
D) Reconciled

Question 44

What does Nancy feel about death?

A) Curiosity
B) Apprehension
C) Fear
D) Anxiety

ANSWERS
Summary & Worked Solutions
Multiple Choice Answer Sheet

Answers

1	B	**16**	B	**31**	D
2	D	**17**	C	**32**	C
3	C	**18**	B	**33**	D
4	D	**19**	D	**34**	C
5	B	**20**	A	**35**	B
6	A	**21**	C	**36**	C
7	D	**22**	C	**37**	B
8	B	**23**	B	**38**	D
9	A	**24**	C	**39**	A
10	A	**25**	B	**40**	C
11	D	**26**	D	**41**	B
12	B	**27**	A	**42**	C
13	A	**28**	A	**43**	D
14	D	**29**	A	**44**	B
15	A	**30**	A		

A = 11
B = 12
C = 10
D = 11

Fully worked solutions

Question 1

B

The doctor in this scenario behaves in an extremely selfish and greedy manner towards the elderly father. When he thinks the son is a lawyer he backtracks and becomes accommodating. This is self-serving behaviour in both cases. He is not quite being self-protective as though he backtracks his initial behaviour is self–serving and in changing he maintains this attitude.

Question 2

D

The son is there to support and provide a voice for his father who is quite vulnerable. In this, he is taking the role of an advocate – a person who provides support for another who requires protection on account of a weakness.

Question 3

C

There is not enough in the stimulus to 'read into' it that the doctor is afraid of being sued or will somehow get into legal trouble – even though his behaviour has been immoral and unethical. Thus B and D must be ruled out. In terms of the actual scenario it cannot be assumed that the doctor has 'met his match' – indeed, if anything, the doctor's change suggests he thinks he is smarter and can adapt to the changing circumstances. However, he may also feel a little disconcerted.

Clearly though, the change in doctor's behaviour comes about because he is led to believe that the son is a legal expert.

Question 4

D

The mother clearly defines success by external measures. As the eldest son is in a selective school this makes her feel he 'has made it'. In this context her other children, she believes should be like him. Hence D is clearly correct.

Question 5

B

The mother's English may be fine however, she believes that her own command of English is so poor that she cannot have her son read to him. She is quite certain about this, hence both A and D cannot be correct. It is more correct to say that she would feel under-confident rather than useless.

Question 6

A

The mother here is focused on 'hard work' as the answer to underachievement. Anything that challenges this belief would be quite confronting. The issue of cost and affordability did not arise hence both B and C can be removed from possible consideration. There is nothing in the text to suggest that trust was an issue. However, there is much to indicate that the mother wants, more than anything, for her son to be smart. Hence A is the best response.

Question 7

D

The author is clearly an advocate for the boy and wants the mother to understand that he has a learning difficulty and needs support. Thus, the mother deciding to avoid giving her son support would represent a huge loss for the boy. Hence D is correct.

Question 8

B

Throughout this conversation Mark sounds skeptical and needing reassurance. Thus the best characterisation of his feeling would be confused and uncertain.

Question 9

A

Josie is a woman who likes to set her boundaries and then decide if, and when, to lower them. That she even articulates this means that she trusts Mark and is therefore not too guarded to get close. Moreover, that she says 'might' indicates she does not really want to feel vulnerable. Hence B and D are incorrect. There is nothing to suggest that she does not want to hurt Mark – the comment is too self-focused. Hence A is correct.

Question 10

A

D is clearly incorrect. The term 'spirited' implies free from tension but also robust. However, there is some name calling: 'lazy' and 'idiot'. However, neither of the parties is angry. Hence, the best characterisation would be 'tense'.

Question 11

D

Indolent means lazy, or inclined to lethargy. This is more accurate than the word sleepy – which can mean tired as well. Thus D is the correct response.

Question 12

B

Greig is clearly a man who challenges assumptions and is strong enough to define himself. Since he is active and strong neither A nor D are likely quotes and they can be eliminated from consideration. Between B and C, B is the better response as there is not anything in the text to suggest that Greig is driven to point of extremes. After all he does say, "things can be underdone and they can be overdone..." suggesting that he has a sense of balance and will set goals that are tough but achievable.

Question 13

A

Anger is a 'secondary emotion' and usually there are underlying primary emotions behind it. Since anger is often an attempt to regain control then the primary emotion is one of loss of control as per A. B and C and clearly incorrect and there is nothing in the text to suggest that the author was predicting future sieges – hence D can also be discounted.

Question 14

D

For the author to catch her breath, the feelings are very strong. There is no anxiety indicated so C is incorrect. Whilst the author may feel a loss of some kind of innocence and sadness associated with that loss, the best response is overwhelmed as, a month later, she still catches her breath. Thus D is the best of the remaining responses.

Question 15

A

Sombre means gloomy, solemn or depressing and thus is associated with negative feeling such as melancholy, sober (serious or grave) and mournful. Effusive means bubbly and enthusiastic and is thus correct as it is NOT an appropriate alternative word.

Question 16

B

Sam sounds misplaced and looking for meaningful work. He also feels a bit stuck. Thus he would not feel angry or lonely. Sadness, like 'happy' and 'angry' can be characterised as a secondary emotion. The primary emotion, and the more relevant answer is that Sam is feeling dispirited. The work he does is demeaning (some times called 'soul destroying') and dispiriting. Hence B is correct.

Question 17

C

Sam has already done retail work so it would not represent a reality check and A can be discounted. Sam characterised retail as 'better pay and less demeaning', which means that he does not see it as 'exciting' or as an 'opportunity.' Rather, it is seen as an escape from the present work he is doing.

Question 18

B

There is nothing to suggest that the situation described was fraught with lies hence A is not correct. Questions carry a certain restlessness, thus the questions do not really represent a search for calmness but rather a search for understanding.

Question 19

D

Rain often evokes feeling of sadness – grey skies, darkness (clouds masking the sunlight) and people seeking the solace and protection of shelter. Hence C is too extreme to be correct but D takes the correct interpretation. As regards A: the author does not seek to 'wash away' the relationship. Indeed, in seeking answers there is an implied need to reconcile the disjunct with the relationship breakup. As regards B: there does not sound like there is any uncertainty – the relationship is over. The author just needs to come to terms with that.

Question 20

A

The author understands his ex-partner's past and would not want her to experience that situation again. This is both protective and compassionate – however, as the relationship has ended and this is reflective, it cannot be protective in the sense of the time and hence is far more a compassionate reflection (especially in the context of the paragraph). As regards B: whilst the author is seeking to distinguishing himself from his ex-partner's previous experiences – it is not a feeling evoked by the line. In terms of C: the author may feel hurt but the depth of feeling is greater and more subtle.

Question 21

C

Given the age of Nora's children and the overly close communications there are unnaturally dependent relationships between her and her children – hence, though there is undoubted care and love – the parenting style is controlling and mutually dependent.

Question 22

C

Pinky may be classified as each of the words presented. Thus there is a need to understand where her sentiment lies. Is she antagonistic or does she want Nora to grow out of her dependencies? She seems to be an advocate for the women's children (characterising them correctly as 'women' rather than 'girls'). She also appears to be trying to get Nora to see the broader effects of her dependency on her work. In this regard and given the context, the best word would be passionate – with observant a close second!

Question 23

B

Nora throughout shows no real openness to change and is very certain of herself. Thus C can be discounted from consideration. If Nora is feeling attacked or pressured then her response will be to defend herself. Hence B is the best answer since it aptly subsumes both A and D.

Question 24

C

There is nothing to suggest that Adam is confident in a situation where cars crash hence A must be incorrect. He does not act with numbness as he responds quickly to the situation, hence D is also incorrect. He runs to the accident – thus there is no ambivalence at all. He does say that he 'feared the worst' whilst he worked for the best. Thus there would be fear and also trepidation as to whether he could make a difference and how the situation might turn out. Thus C is correct.

Question 25

B

He states that he was 'lucky to be alive' thus relief is the best response and B is correct.

Question 26

D

Brent does not seem passive – his statements are consistent with a person who has strength and insight about himself and also his sister. Thus C is not correct. Brent cannot be classified as reactive – he is far too insightful, thus B is also incorrect. As regards Zephyr – she sounds more persistent (repeating the same thing about the present on three occasions) than inquisitive – hence D is correct.

Question 27

A

Of all the alternatives, D can be discounted straight away as there is nothing to suggest that Zephyr forgot. Indeed that she called indicates she remembered the birthday. Brent does not sound in need of help thus C is also incorrect. Now of A and B – if Zephyr was keen to do the right thing by Brent then she would not have asked the question about what he wanted, or thrown it to him to request a present. Thus B cannot really be correct. Underneath, the subtext is that Zephyr just wants Brett to know that she is thinking of him. Hence A is correct.

Question 28

A

Brent does not come across as either angry or sad hence C and D can be eliminated. He is not feeling objectified – but his reference to having said the same thing on previous occasions does indicate that he feels unheard and hence undervalued. Thus A is correct.

Question 29

A

Since Lydia has mixed feelings – both of happiness and also that the system is complex and time consuming, then the best response is ambivalent. Ambivalence means feeling mixed or opposing feeling simultaneously.

Question 30

A

This is an interesting question, because whilst Lydia might hear the name calling ('pushy parent') she feels that this is discriminatory and that she is treated differently (she does not belong and it viewed with suspicion) on account of her advocacy. Clearly, since she does not get unqualified support or total exclusion both B and D must be incorrect.

Question 31

D

Since her daughter is entirely dependent upon her, Lydia must advocate on behalf of her daughter. She is strong in doing so and thus B is obviously wrong. She does not accept the situation as she wants her daughter to get an appropriate education thus she is not 'surprisingly accepting' and C is also incorrect. There is nothing to suggest that she is 'surprisingly' forthright (this respond may suggest some sort of gender discrimination – women and men can both be strong advocates – so what is the 'surprise'?) thus D is the best and most appropriate response.

Question 32

C

Helga recounts that she is 'not sure how' Ophelia will cope and thus she is clearly uncertain so C is the best response.

Question 33

D

Helga sounds concerned about Terrence not being seen and she is keen to ensure that this does not happen. She is therefore watchful of the situation and D is the best answer.

Question 34

C

Helga is clearly not hopeless as she is aware of her children each as individuals, as well as herself and her work situation in trying to balance time with children and work. Hence B is incorrect as is A. Whilst her situation is limiting Helga would view it as restrictive – because she cannot balance all of the competing demands on her given time and financial constraints.

Question 35

B

Josette is not against breastfeeding – she is against the notion of a child being breastfed in public. Thus C and D can be ruled out as they are incorrect. Josette seems to think that breastfeeding in public lowers a woman's elf-respect not the overall standard of society – thus A is incorrect. B is clearly therefore correct and, in fact, is exactly what she says in her fourth statement.

Question 36

C

When a person invokes an invisible majority to support an argument then they are seeking reinforcement of a point of view through the validation of some external standard or widely held norm. Thus C is correct here.

Question 37

B

Debbie is certainly not flippant but she is thoughtful and passionate. Thus A cannot be correct. She is clearly a caring person – but what is her concern? Throughout the discussion she maintains her interest in the main issue – that of breastfeeding in public – and that women should not feel shamed into doing otherwise. Thus she is very focused and persuasive. She does not come across as aggressive – though Josette does. Hence B is the best response in terms of Debbie's tone and language.

Question 38

D

There is nothing in the text to suggest that the author thinks men should hide their pain as a fact of gender thus A and C both must be incorrect. Nor is there anything in the text to suggest that hiding pain is required in order to win. He does however state that an opponent will exploit a perceived weakness and that showing pain may lead to an opponent exploiting that. Hence D is correct.

Question 39

A

The text is an interesting insight into the world of an elite sporting professional. It may be helpful to some people but it's intention is to give insight – thus B cannot be totally correct and C is clearly plain wrong. Whilst the recount does imply the sportsman is quite intuitive (he can read his body) the best answer is A because to manage pain and also compete at a very high level of competition must take exceptional determination. Hence A is correct.

Question 40

C

There is nothing in the text to suggest that losing is painful thus A is not correct. There is also nothing that indicates the management of pain is the goal. Rather the management of pain is necessary if the actual goal of successfully competing is to be achieved. Hence B is incorrect and C is correct. In terms of D: It is not a necessary fact of competition that there must be pain even though the sportsman's experience was that he usually carried some pain ('niggle' or injury) hence D must be incorrect.

Question 41

B

She would certainly not have felt either delighted or satisfied – hence A and C are not correct. She was probably disappointed with herself but in terms of the context she would have felt exposed, as the person about whom the email was centred would have read it, seen how she was perceived by Tickie and would have seen a side to Tickie she may not have been aware of. Thus Tickie would have felt exposed and B is correct.

Question 42

C

Betty takes on different roles – first teasing ('a beautiful mess'), then calling Tickie mean. However she backtracks when she says, 'you owe her no apologies'. In a way, people like Betty give very mixed messages and would be extremely unhelpful as she keeps changing with respect to Tickie. Thus she is neither supportive nor critical – displaying elements of both. She is also far from neutral. Thus the best answer is confusing and C is correct. (NB: Avoid such people☺)

Question 43

D

Nancy sounds quite resolved about her life as she feels 'satisfaction' that her children are happy and have not suffered as a result of her parenting. Thus she is not regretful or restless. The term 'reassured' is not really relevant – thus D – reconciled – is correct.

Question 44

B

Nancy does not express that she is curious or afraid – thus A and C are incorrect. She does not sound anxious but she does sound a bit apprehensive as she is unsure exactly how death will come. The questions do not indicate anxiety but something less stressed and more open. Thus B is correct.

Notes

Notes

Notes

Notes

Notes

Essential Preparation for

UMAT

UNDERGRADUATE MEDICINE & HEALTH SCIENCES ADMISSION TEST

MULTIPLE CHOICE ANSWER SHEET

Use pencil when filling out this sheet

Fill in the circle correctly

| ● | Ⓑ | Ⓒ | Ⓓ |

If you make a mistake neatly cross it out and circle the correct response

| ⊗ | ● | Ⓒ | Ⓓ |

1 Ⓐ Ⓑ Ⓒ Ⓓ   23 Ⓐ Ⓑ Ⓒ Ⓓ

2 Ⓐ Ⓑ Ⓒ Ⓓ   24 Ⓐ Ⓑ Ⓒ Ⓓ

3 Ⓐ Ⓑ Ⓒ Ⓓ   25 Ⓐ Ⓑ Ⓒ Ⓓ

4 Ⓐ Ⓑ Ⓒ Ⓓ   26 Ⓐ Ⓑ Ⓒ Ⓓ

5 Ⓐ Ⓑ Ⓒ Ⓓ   27 Ⓐ Ⓑ Ⓒ Ⓓ

6 Ⓐ Ⓑ Ⓒ Ⓓ   28 Ⓐ Ⓑ Ⓒ Ⓓ

7 Ⓐ Ⓑ Ⓒ Ⓓ   29 Ⓐ Ⓑ Ⓒ Ⓓ

8 Ⓐ Ⓑ Ⓒ Ⓓ   30 Ⓐ Ⓑ Ⓒ Ⓓ

9 Ⓐ Ⓑ Ⓒ Ⓓ   31 Ⓐ Ⓑ Ⓒ Ⓓ

10 Ⓐ Ⓑ Ⓒ Ⓓ   32 Ⓐ Ⓑ Ⓒ Ⓓ

11 Ⓐ Ⓑ Ⓒ Ⓓ   33 Ⓐ Ⓑ Ⓒ Ⓓ

12 Ⓐ Ⓑ Ⓒ Ⓓ   34 Ⓐ Ⓑ Ⓒ Ⓓ

13 Ⓐ Ⓑ Ⓒ Ⓓ   35 Ⓐ Ⓑ Ⓒ Ⓓ

14 Ⓐ Ⓑ Ⓒ Ⓓ   36 Ⓐ Ⓑ Ⓒ Ⓓ

15 Ⓐ Ⓑ Ⓒ Ⓓ   37 Ⓐ Ⓑ Ⓒ Ⓓ

16 Ⓐ Ⓑ Ⓒ Ⓓ   38 Ⓐ Ⓑ Ⓒ Ⓓ

17 Ⓐ Ⓑ Ⓒ Ⓓ   39 Ⓐ Ⓑ Ⓒ Ⓓ

18 Ⓐ Ⓑ Ⓒ Ⓓ   40 Ⓐ Ⓑ Ⓒ Ⓓ

19 Ⓐ Ⓑ Ⓒ Ⓓ   41 Ⓐ Ⓑ Ⓒ Ⓓ

20 Ⓐ Ⓑ Ⓒ Ⓓ   42 Ⓐ Ⓑ Ⓒ Ⓓ

21 Ⓐ Ⓑ Ⓒ Ⓓ   43 Ⓐ Ⓑ Ⓒ Ⓓ

22 Ⓐ Ⓑ Ⓒ Ⓓ   44 Ⓐ Ⓑ Ⓒ Ⓓ

48

Essential Preparation for

UMAT

UNDERGRADUATE MEDICINE & HEALTH SCIENCES ADMISSION TEST

MULTIPLE CHOICE ANSWER SHEET

Use pencil when filling out this sheet

Fill in the circle correctly			
●	Ⓑ	Ⓒ	Ⓓ

If you make a mistake neatly cross it out and circle the correct response			
⊗	●	Ⓒ	Ⓓ

1 Ⓐ Ⓑ Ⓒ Ⓓ   23 Ⓐ Ⓑ Ⓒ Ⓓ

2 Ⓐ Ⓑ Ⓒ Ⓓ   24 Ⓐ Ⓑ Ⓒ Ⓓ

3 Ⓐ Ⓑ Ⓒ Ⓓ   25 Ⓐ Ⓑ Ⓒ Ⓓ

4 Ⓐ Ⓑ Ⓒ Ⓓ   26 Ⓐ Ⓑ Ⓒ Ⓓ

5 Ⓐ Ⓑ Ⓒ Ⓓ   27 Ⓐ Ⓑ Ⓒ Ⓓ

6 Ⓐ Ⓑ Ⓒ Ⓓ   28 Ⓐ Ⓑ Ⓒ Ⓓ

7 Ⓐ Ⓑ Ⓒ Ⓓ   29 Ⓐ Ⓑ Ⓒ Ⓓ

8 Ⓐ Ⓑ Ⓒ Ⓓ   30 Ⓐ Ⓑ Ⓒ Ⓓ

9 Ⓐ Ⓑ Ⓒ Ⓓ   31 Ⓐ Ⓑ Ⓒ Ⓓ

10 Ⓐ Ⓑ Ⓒ Ⓓ   32 Ⓐ Ⓑ Ⓒ Ⓓ

11 Ⓐ Ⓑ Ⓒ Ⓓ   33 Ⓐ Ⓑ Ⓒ Ⓓ

12 Ⓐ Ⓑ Ⓒ Ⓓ   34 Ⓐ Ⓑ Ⓒ Ⓓ

13 Ⓐ Ⓑ Ⓒ Ⓓ   35 Ⓐ Ⓑ Ⓒ Ⓓ

14 Ⓐ Ⓑ Ⓒ Ⓓ   36 Ⓐ Ⓑ Ⓒ Ⓓ

15 Ⓐ Ⓑ Ⓒ Ⓓ   37 Ⓐ Ⓑ Ⓒ Ⓓ

16 Ⓐ Ⓑ Ⓒ Ⓓ   38 Ⓐ Ⓑ Ⓒ Ⓓ

17 Ⓐ Ⓑ Ⓒ Ⓓ   39 Ⓐ Ⓑ Ⓒ Ⓓ

18 Ⓐ Ⓑ Ⓒ Ⓓ   40 Ⓐ Ⓑ Ⓒ Ⓓ

19 Ⓐ Ⓑ Ⓒ Ⓓ   41 Ⓐ Ⓑ Ⓒ Ⓓ

20 Ⓐ Ⓑ Ⓒ Ⓓ   42 Ⓐ Ⓑ Ⓒ Ⓓ

21 Ⓐ Ⓑ Ⓒ Ⓓ   43 Ⓐ Ⓑ Ⓒ Ⓓ

22 Ⓐ Ⓑ Ⓒ Ⓓ   44 Ⓐ Ⓑ Ⓒ Ⓓ

Essential Preparation for

UMAT

UNDERGRADUATE MEDICINE & HEALTH SCIENCES ADMISSION TEST

MULTIPLE CHOICE ANSWER SHEET

Use pencil when filling out this sheet

Fill in the circle correctly			
●	B	C	D

If you make a mistake neatly cross it out and circle the correct response			
⊗	●	C	D

1 (A) (B) (C) (D)
2 (A) (B) (C) (D)
3 (A) (B) (C) (D)
4 (A) (B) (C) (D)
5 (A) (B) (C) (D)
6 (A) (B) (C) (D)
7 (A) (B) (C) (D)
8 (A) (B) (C) (D)
9 (A) (B) (C) (D)
10 (A) (B) (C) (D)
11 (A) (B) (C) (D)
12 (A) (B) (C) (D)
13 (A) (B) (C) (D)
14 (A) (B) (C) (D)
15 (A) (B) (C) (D)
16 (A) (B) (C) (D)
17 (A) (B) (C) (D)
18 (A) (B) (C) (D)
19 (A) (B) (C) (D)
20 (A) (B) (C) (D)
21 (A) (B) (C) (D)
22 (A) (B) (C) (D)

23 (A) (B) (C) (D)
24 (A) (B) (C) (D)
25 (A) (B) (C) (D)
26 (A) (B) (C) (D)
27 (A) (B) (C) (D)
28 (A) (B) (C) (D)
29 (A) (B) (C) (D)
30 (A) (B) (C) (D)
31 (A) (B) (C) (D)
32 (A) (B) (C) (D)
33 (A) (B) (C) (D)
34 (A) (B) (C) (D)
35 (A) (B) (C) (D)
36 (A) (B) (C) (D)
37 (A) (B) (C) (D)
38 (A) (B) (C) (D)
39 (A) (B) (C) (D)
40 (A) (B) (C) (D)
41 (A) (B) (C) (D)
42 (A) (B) (C) (D)
43 (A) (B) (C) (D)
44 (A) (B) (C) (D)